DEMCO

The Fall of the Soviet Union

Miles Harvey

 CHILDRENS PRESS®
CHICAGO

Library of Congress Cataloging-in-Publication Data

Harvey, Miles.
    The fall of the Soviet Union/by Miles Harvey.
        p. cm.–(Cornerstones of freedom)
    ISBN 0-516-06694-3
    1. Soviet Union—History—Juvenile literature. 2. Former
Soviet republics—History—Juvenile literature. [1. Soviet
Union—History. 2. Former Soviet republics—History.]
I. Title. II. Series.
DK266.H364 1995
947—dc20   94-24371
                                              CIP
                                              AC

On December 25, 1991, a huge red flag was lowered from its flagpole over the city of Moscow. As the flag came down, one of the most important countries in world history came to an end.

The flag was the emblem of the Union of Soviet Socialist Republics (USSR), more commonly known as the Soviet Union. Just a few months earlier, the Soviet Union had been a country of 280 million people and covered more than twice as much land as the United States. Now it was breaking up into fifteen separate countries.

Above: The Soviet flag
Below: The Kremlin in Moscow, capital of the former Soviet Union

A crowd runs from gunfire in the revolution of 1917. In 1917, the people revolted and overthrew the czar of Russia.

"We are now living in a new world," said Mikhail Gorbachev, the final Soviet leader. He was correct. The Soviet Union's rise and fall is one of the most important stories of the twentieth century.

The story began more than seventy years earlier in Russia, a vast country that spans much of Europe and Asia. Before 1917, Russia was ruled by an emperor known as the *czar*. But in 1917, the Russian people rose up against the czar and revolted.

Why were these people so angry at their ruler? One reason was that the majority of Russians were very poor. That's because the czar and a small number of rich people owned most of the land and businesses in Russia. Many people wanted to make Russian society more fair for everyone. Some thought a system called socialism was the way to do it.

Socialists believe that a society's money and property should be divided evenly among the citizens. They think it's wrong for some people to have more wealth than they need, while others are so poor they can't afford adequate food, clothes, and shelter.

In the early 1900s, many Russians were peasants whose families had been poor for generations.

Czar Nicholas II

There are many different kinds of socialists. A lot of socialists are in favor of giving all citizens the right to vote. But in Russia, one group of socialists—called communists—thought that a small group of government officials should make all the decisions for the country.

Under pressure from the people, Czar Nicholas II gave up power in 1917, and his government fell. In the following years, communists rose to power in Russia. Their leader was named Vladimir Lenin. He became the country's new ruler, and Russia became the first communist country ever to exist.

Vladimir Lenin

Many people around the world dreamed that Lenin and the communists could transform Russia into an "ideal" society. They hoped that communism would do away with poverty, injustice, and crime. But things did not work out that way.

Lenin believed in using force to get things done. He imprisoned or murdered thousands of his opponents. He outlawed any newspapers or magazines that criticized his plans. And he tried to discourage religion.

Lenin (center) strolls through Moscow's Red Square in 1919.

Some Russian factory workers and farm-workers thought communism would mean that they would own their own land or run their own businesses. But that didn't happen. Instead, the communist government confiscated the farms and factories. It even took grain needed for bread and other foods from poor people. And it forced everyone to work for the government.

Lenin helped communists in several neighboring regions to take power. In 1922, these areas joined with Russia to form the Soviet Union.

The Soviet Union (USSR) dominated eastern Europe and much of Asia.

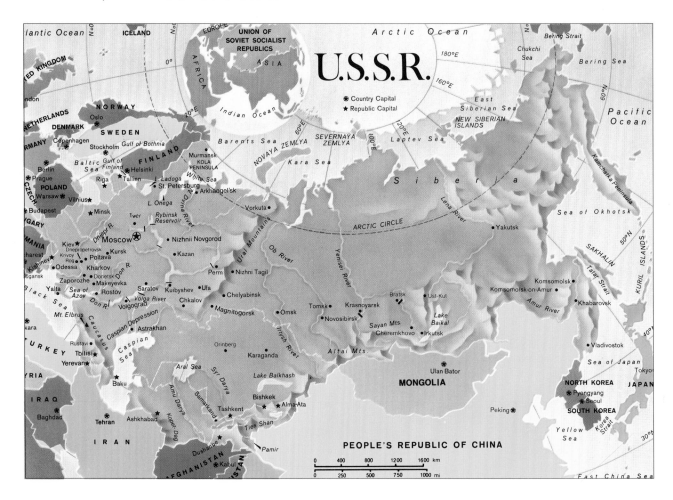

Many Russians lived in poor conditions and were near starvation (left) under the rule of Joseph Stalin (right).

In 1924, Lenin died. The new Soviet leader was even more cruel than Lenin. His name was Joseph Stalin. Stalin ruled the country for the next three decades. During that time, an estimated 25 million Soviet people were killed by their own government or died of starvation as a result of Stalin's programs.

Under Stalin, the Soviet Union further expanded its borders. New republics joined the union as the Soviet empire crept into Asia and Europe.

During World War II, Stalin (seated, right) was allied with Great Britain's Winston Churchill (left) and U.S. president Franklin D. Roosevelt (center).

The Soviet Union began World War II (1939–45) on the same side as Nazi Germany. But when Germany invaded the Soviet Union, Stalin switched sides and joined forces with the Allies, led by England and the United States. Together, the Allies crushed their enemies and won the war. But the United States and the Soviet Union didn't remain friendly for long.

After the war, Stalin cut off the Soviet Union from trade and communication with most of the West. British prime minister Winston Churchill described the Soviets as being isolated behind an "iron curtain."

In the 1950s, the Soviets seized control of countries throughout Eastern Europe. Democratic countries in the West feared that communism would spread and take over Europe completely. In 1949, the United States, England, France, and several other countries formed the North Atlantic Treaty Organization (NATO). The main purpose of NATO was to establish a military force to defend against attacks by the Soviet Union. In 1955, the Soviet Union formed a similar union with the communist governments of Albania, Bulgaria, Czechoslovakia, East Germany, Hungary, Poland, and Romania. This agreement was called the Warsaw Pact.

In the years after World War II, the Soviets built a huge and powerful military.

The United States and the Soviet Union were the largest and most powerful of the NATO and Warsaw Pact countries. So these two "superpowers" feuded for more than forty years, from the mid-1940s into the 1980s. Their conflict was known as the "cold war." A "hot war" is one in which countries' militaries are engaged in battle. But there were no actual battles between U.S. and Soviet forces. Soviet and American leaders used the threat of warfare to hopefully avoid a real war.

The superpowers engaged in an arms race, spending billions of dollars to build up their military forces. Thousands of nuclear weapons were built. The missiles could be launched at a moment's notice. The explosion of a single nuclear warhead can wipe out an entire city. Both nations had enough nuclear weapons to destroy the entire planet many times over. In the 1950s and '60s, the threat of global nuclear war was a real and frightening possibility.

The United States and the Soviet Union came closest to actual warfare during the Cuban missile crisis of 1962. Cuba, an island nation off the coast of Florida, was heavily influenced by the Soviet Union. The Soviets used this influence to install nuclear missiles on Cuban soil. When U.S. spy planes discovered these missiles, President John F. Kennedy confronted the Soviet government. Kennedy demanded that the missiles be removed, but the Soviets refused. Several tense weeks followed as the two countries were locked in a standoff. Both sides had their militaries on full alert, and the world wondered if the superpowers would begin launching missiles at one another. In the end, the Soviet Union backed down, thus avoiding disaster.

Meanwhile, life under communism continued to be difficult for Soviet citizens. Stalin had died in 1953. The Soviet leaders who followed during the next three decades were not quite as brutal as Stalin, but living conditions were still awful. Soviet citizens had none of the liberties Americans take for granted, such as the right to free speech, the right to vote in elections, and even the right to practice a religion. If Soviet citizens didn't like these conditions, they were not allowed to leave the country. And if they were discovered writing articles or speaking out against the government, they were sent to huge, faraway prisons known as *gulags*.

The Soviet newspaper Pravda *shows a photograph of Stalin's funeral.*

Even so, not all Soviets hated the communist system. Some people liked the fact that they were guaranteed jobs and free health care, for example. But to many citizens, these advantages were outweighed by the deplorable living conditions and the lack of individual liberties. As the years went on, more and more Soviets became fed up with their government. People were becoming convinced that their country needed new leaders and a new system. Even many government officials realized that there had to be a change.

The chance for change arrived in 1985, when Soviet leader Konstantin Chernenko died. To replace him, communist officials selected a man named Mikhail Gorbachev. Not many people outside the Soviet Union had heard of Gorbachev. But in the next five years, he would become a hero around the world.

As soon as Gorbachev took control, the Soviet people realized they were getting a different kind of leader. At age fifty-four, Gorbachev was one of the youngest men ever to lead the country. And unlike previous leaders, he seemed genuinely interested in the Soviet people's concerns. He and his wife, Raisa, would sometimes stop on the street and talk to ordinary Soviet citizens. "I'm listening to you," Gorbachev assured the crowds.

The new Soviet leader encouraged *perestroika,* the Russian word for "restructuring." Gorbachev used that word because he wanted to restructure Soviet society in all areas—its economy, industry, foreign relations, and its attitudes toward human rights.

Gorbachev also called for *glasnost,* which means "openness" in Russian. He wanted to open Soviet society so that people wouldn't be afraid to express their opinions. To prove that he was serious, Gorbachev released dozens of people who were in jail because of things they had said or written against the Soviet government.

In the late 1980s, Mikhail Gorbachev and wife Raisa became immensely popular figures around the world.

Gorbachev revised the Soviet economy so that businesses from the West, such as McDonald's (right), could enter the USSR. American merchandise was sold in Soviet stores, such as the huge GUM Department Store in Moscow (below, left). Many Soviet people went into business for themselves, like this woman selling vegetables (below, right).

Gorbachev's ideas caught on quickly. People believed he was truly interested in transforming the Soviet Union into a more democratic society. Soviet journalists were free to report honestly about the country's problems. Artists, filmmakers, musicians, novelists, and poets began creating exciting new works. People could practice their own religions. If they wanted to leave the Soviet Union, they were given permission.

Gorbachev hoped to revitalize the Soviet economy by allowing a free market. Many Soviet citizens chose to start their own businesses rather than work for the government. And foreign companies began to set up stores and factories in the Soviet Union. Even a McDonald's restaurant opened in Moscow.

By late 1989, Gorbachev's influence had spread like wildfire across Eastern Europe. The Warsaw Pact crumbled. People from communist countries demanded that their governments allow them more freedom. In Poland, the government agreed to hold free elections. It was the first time any communist government in Eastern Europe had agreed to allow an election in which all parties had a fair chance. What happened next was even more amazing: the communists lost. For the first time, a communist government gave up control peacefully.

Demonstrators in Prague, Czechoslovakia, celebrate the fall of their communist government in 1989.

As 1989 drew to a close, the people also overthrew the communist governments of Czechoslovakia, East Germany, Romania, and Hungary. In the past, the Soviet Union would have sent tanks and troops to stomp out these revolutions. But now, Mikhail Gorbachev stood by and allowed Eastern Europeans to decide their own fates. "We have no right...to interfere in the events happening there," he said.

Perhaps the most dramatic event of this period was the opening of the Berlin Wall on November 11, 1989. For twenty-seven years, the Wall had divided East and West Germany. It stood as a symbol of the separation between the communist countries of the East and the democratic countries of the West. When the Wall was dismantled and Germany was reunited in early 1990, the world reacted with astonishment and joy. Freedom was finally winning in Eastern Europe.

People were even more surprised as Mikhail Gorbachev negotiated with the United States to end the forty-year cold war. In 1987, Gorbachev and U.S. president Ronald Reagan signed a treaty aimed at reducing their stores of nuclear weapons. Several more summit meetings were held and more agreements were made. In December 1989, Gorbachev met with the new U.S. president, George Bush, aboard a Soviet battleship off the coast of Malta. At that meeting, the leaders agreed to further arms reductions and to remove troops from threatening positions in Europe. The United States also pledged to assist Gorbachev in his attempt to revitalize the Soviet economy. The happy leaders emerged from the meeting with amazing news. They declared that the cold war was over. President Bush said that the two countries were entering "a brand-new era of U.S.-Soviet relations."

George Bush and Mikhail Gorbachev seal an arms reduction agreement with a joyous handshake.

Mikhail Gorbachev negotiated an end to the cold war with the United States, and thousands of nuclear missiles (above) were then dismantled.

Mikhail Gorbachev was now being praised as one of the most important political figures of the century. The changes he brought about had been unthinkable just a few years before. In 1990, he won the Nobel Peace Prize, the highest honor a world leader can receive.

Despite Gorbachev's fame and success, however, not everything was going well at home. Change was coming very slowly, and the Soviet economy was struggling. Gorbachev knew he could not expect to change the country's economy overnight, so he did not want to abandon socialism entirely.

But there were others in the Soviet government who disagreed with Gorbachev. One of his strongest critics was Boris Yeltsin. Yeltsin wanted the Soviet Union's reforms to move ahead more quickly. He also wanted the main government to give up power so that each region of the Soviet Union could become an independent country—including Russia, where Yeltsin was the top politician.

Other Soviet leaders were dissatisfied with Gorbachev for the opposite reason. These leaders were old-fashioned communists. They thought Gorbachev was making too many changes too fast. They wanted to return the Soviet Union to the way it was before the days of glasnost and perestroika.

Many of these "hard-line" communists were members of the military and the secret police. These men were accustomed to getting what they wanted through intimidation and violent force. In August 1991, they decided that Gorbachev had to be stopped. They came up with a plan to remove him from office and take control of the government.

Boris Yeltsin

On August 18, 1991, while Gorbachev was away from the Soviet capital of Moscow on vacation, the communist leaders put their plan into action. They took over radio and television stations. They sent tanks and troops into the streets of the city. They announced that Gorbachev was unable to be president because of "health reasons." That was a lie, of course. Gorbachev wasn't sick at all. In fact, the leaders of the revolt were holding him hostage.

When hard-line communist leaders attempted to oust Gorbachev, they called out tanks to secure the streets of Moscow (right). But crowds of Russians filled the streets (below) and blocked the military advance. The people repelled the communist takeover without violence or bloodshed.

But their attempt to grab power was not as easy as they thought it would be. Thousands of people flooded the streets of Moscow and other Soviet cities to protest Gorbachev's removal. Ironically, these demonstrators were led by Gorbachev's rival, Boris Yeltsin.

Why did Yeltsin help Gorbachev? The answer is simple. Yeltsin knew that if the communist leaders took power, they would try to overturn *all* the country's recent changes. Although Yeltsin and Gorbachev disagreed about many things, they both believed strongly in getting rid of the old system.

"Aggression will not go forward!" Yeltsin told the protesters. "Only democracy will win!"

Boris Yeltsin commandeered a tank, stood on it, and read an inspiring speech to the people of Moscow. He declared, "Only democracy will win!"

Boris Yeltsin (left) and Mikhail Gorbachev (right)

Yeltsin turned out to be right. The demonstrators stopped the communist revolt from gaining full control of the government. The leaders of the revolt had tanks and troops on their side, so they could have crushed the protesters easily. But television cameras would have broadcast this bloodshed to the world, so the leaders of the revolt backed down. They finally gave up on August 21.

Mikhail Gorbachev returned to Moscow and thanked Boris Yeltsin for helping to stop the takeover. Gorbachev explained the Soviet people's support of him, saying that they had "breathed the air of freedom, and nobody can take that away from them any longer."

Within days, the Soviet Union began to fall apart. First, Gorbachev quit as the head of the Communist Party, the group that had ruled the country since the days of Lenin.

At the same time, the many regions of the country began to declare independence from the Soviet Union. The Soviet Union eventually split into fifteen different countries. Boris Yeltsin became the head of Russia, the largest of those lands. Eleven of the countries, including Russia, formed an organization called the Commonwealth of Independent States, which was designed to help the new nations work together on various projects.

With the Soviet Union no longer in existence, there was no need for a Soviet leader. That meant that Mikhail Gorbachev was out of a job. On December 25, 1991, he resigned. On that day, the Soviet Union officially came to an end.

Above: Mikhail Gorbachev officially resigns from office. Below: In 1991, the Soviet Union split into several different republics. The largest is Russia.

The Russian economy has struggled, and people in the former Soviet Union have suffered from an increase in crime.

And what has happened since the Soviet Union's collapse? Some good things and some bad things. There is, of course, more freedom than there used to be. People can express their views without fear. They can freely read books, watch TV shows, buy products, open businesses, and do many other things that were banned in the Soviet Union. Nonetheless, many former Soviet citizens have found it hard to adjust to the new world that they live in.

One big problem is money. In the old Soviet Union, the government ran all the businesses. This had many disadvantages, but it also meant that almost everybody was guaranteed a job. Now there are no guarantees. In Russia, for example, some people have grown rich, but many Russians are worse off financially than they had been under communism. A lot of people have resorted to crime to make a living.

Much of this criminal activity takes place in gangster-style mobs. According to some estimates, two out of every three businesses in Russia are involved in some kind of illegal activity.

One reason for the economic problems is that so many of the old government-run factories specialized in making military equipment. Because the cold war with the United States is over, most of this equipment is no longer needed. And many factories that made nonmilitary products have old and poorly designed equipment. These old factories create another serious problem: air, water, and soil pollution. The Soviet government never told people how serious the country's environmental problems were. Now the truth is coming out.

A Russian farmer works on polluted land near a nuclear power plant's cooling towers.

Slow economic growth has led to long lines and little merchandise in many stores.

Many experts think that these problems—and many more—will be solved with time. They believe that free-market economics eventually will succeed in the former Soviet Union. In a free-market economy, the government steps out of the way and allows private businesses and individuals to take charge. This is the kind of economy that has existed in the United States for centuries.

Many citizens of the former Soviet Union are growing impatient with the slow pace of change. They feel humiliated and angry. They want to blame someone for their troubles. Encouraged by opportunistic politicians, they often blame people from other religions or ethnic groups. This kind of hatred has led to increased violence in former Soviet countries. Some people fear that these tensions could explode into major wars. The frightening aspect of this situation is that there are still numerous nuclear weapons in those countries.

Of course, there is no way to predict the future. The Soviet Union's collapse could bring chaos or calm, bloodshed or brotherhood. As Mikhail Gorbachev said, it truly is "a new world."

A toppled statue of Lenin signifies the collapse of the Soviet Union he founded.

GLOSSARY

arms race

Czar Nicholas II

arms race—when several countries continually construct weapons in order to have a more powerful military than all other countries

cold war—the conflict between the Soviet Union and the United States that lasted from the mid-1940s through the 1980s; military fighting never broke out, but the threat of nuclear war gripped the world during this period

communism—a version of socialism in which the central government maintains strict control over the people; the Soviet Union was a communist society until 1991

confiscate—to take a person's possessions by force

czar—the Russian word for the emperor, or ruler

democracy—a government in which citizens have the freedom and power to create their own laws

glasnost—the Russian word for "openness" used by Mikhail Gorbachev in the late 1980s to describe the new Russian society he hoped to establish

gulag—a Soviet labor camp; a prison

iron curtain—term referring to the isolation of the Soviet Union from the rest of the world

NATO (North Atlantic Treaty Organization) — a group formed in 1949 consisting of democratic countries that formed a military force to defend against the Soviet Union

perestroika—the Russian word for "restructuring," which became the theme of Mikhail Gorbachev's reform of Soviet government

reform—to change; to remove faults of the past and become new and better

socialism—a theory of society in which all wealth and possessions are divided among the people

Warsaw Pact—an agreement made in 1955 among several communist countries to defend against the NATO countries

TIMELINE

March 15
Czar Nicholas II
gives up power

1917

1922 Union of Soviet Socialist Republics
established

November 7
Lenin leads
people's revolt
over Russian
government

1924

Lenin dies;
Joseph Stalin
eventually
takes power

World War II { **1939**

1945

Cold war begins **1946**

NATO forms **1949**

Warsaw Pact **1955**

Cuban missile crisis **1962**

Gorbachev takes
over USSR

1985

1987 Gorbachev & Reagan agree to reduce arms

1988 First Soviet free elections since 1917

1989

Communist
governments
fall in Poland,
Czechoslovakia,
Romania,
Hungary,
East Germany

1990 Reunification of Germany

1991

August 19, 1991
Boris Yeltsin
defies the
communist
revolt

August 18
Communists
attempt revolt to
oust Gorbachev

August 21
Communist
revolt ends

August 24
Gorbachev
resigns from
Communist Party

December 12
Commonwealth
of Independent
States formed

December 25
Gorbachev
resigns as
president;
Soviet Union
ceases to exist

INDEX (**Boldface** *page numbers indicate illustrations.*)

PHOTO CREDITS

Cover, Reuters/Bettmann; 1, AP/Wide World; 2, Reuters/Bettmann; 3 (top), AP/Wide World; 3 (bottom), ©SuperStock, Inc.; 4, Stock Montage, Inc.; 5, Bettmann; 6 (both images), Stock Montage, Inc.; 7, AP/Wide World; 8, Courtesy Grolier, Inc., *The New Book of Knowledge;* 9 (both photos), 10, AP/Wide World; 11, G. Brettnacher/© SuperStock, Inc.; 13, AP/Wide World; 15, UPI/Bettmann; 16 (top), Reuters/Bettmann; 16 (bottom left), S. Vidler/©SuperStock, Inc.; 16 (bottom right), T. Lipton/ ©SuperStock, Inc.; 18, AP/Wide World; 19, Reuters/Bettmann; 20, AP/Wide World; 21, 22 (top), Reuters/Bettmann; 22 (bottom), 23, 24, AP/Wide World; 25 (top), Reuters/Bettmann; 25 (bottom), Courtesy Grolier, Inc., *The New Book of Knowledge;* 26, AP/Wide World; 27, 28 (top left), Reuters/ Bettmann; 28 (top right and bottom left), AP/Wide World; 29, Reuters/Bettmann; 30 (top), G. Brettnacher/© SuperStock, Inc.; 30 (bottom), Stock Montage, Inc.; 31 (top right), AP/Wide World; 31 (center left), UPI/Bettmann; 31 (bottom left), Bettmann

ADDITIONAL PICTURE IDENTIFICATIONS

Cover: *An anti-communist demonstrator waves a Soviet flag from which the hammer and sickle symbol has been cut out. The hammer and sickle was the symbol of the communist Soviet Union.*

Page 1: *Russians swarm over tanks that had been called out during an attempted takeover by hard-line communists.*

Page 2: *A statue of Lenin is removed in Bucharest, Romania after the collapse of Soviet power.*

STAFF

Project Editor: Mark Friedman

Design & Electronic Composition: TJS Design

Photo Editor: Jan Izzo

Cornerstones of Freedom Logo: David Cunningham

ABOUT THE AUTHOR

Miles Harvey is a writer and editor who lives in Chicago. He gets his love of politics from his father, Bob.